A REAL LIFE FAIRY TALE

PRINCESS GRACE KELLY

A REAL LIFE FAIRY TALE

PRINCESS GRACE KELLY

Written by Emberli Pridham

Illustrated by Danilo Cerovic

gatekeeper press™
TAMPA, FLORIDA

A Real Life Fairy Tale Princess Grace Kelly

Published by Gatekeeper Press

7853 Gunn Hwy, Suite 209
Tampa, FL 33626

www.GatekeeperPress.com

Library of Congress Control Number: 2023943612

ISBN (hardcover): 9781662935282

ISBN (paperback): 9781662935299

eISBN: 9781662935305

A global icon. An enduring legacy. As an actress, Grace Kelly was known for her glamour, beauty, and elegance. As a princess, she modeled leadership, philanthropy, and kindness—she lived her life with remarkable purpose in true royal style. Today, Princess Grace continues to inspire us through her timeless fashion influence, and her significant support for the arts, now celebrated through the annual Princess Grace Awards for emerging talent of extraordinary promise. I am delighted to share Emberli Pridham's book that so beautifully highlights Princess Grace's legacy and showcases the change and positive impact that one person can bring to the world.

– Brisa Carleton, CEO of the Princess Grace Foundation - USA

A global icon. An enduring legacy. As an actress, Grace Kelly was known for her glamour, beauty, and elegance. As a princess, she modeled leadership, philanthropy, and kindness—she lived her life with remarkable purpose in true royal style. Today, Princess Grace continues to inspire us through her timeless fashion influence, and her significant support for the arts, now celebrated through the annual Princess Grace Awards for emerging talent of extraordinary promise. I am delighted to share Emberli Pridham's book that so beautifully highlights Princess Grace's legacy and showcases the change and positive impact that one person can bring to the world.

– Brisa Carleton, CEO of the Princess Grace Foundation - USA

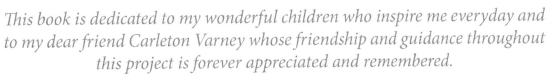

This book is dedicated to my wonderful children who inspire me everyday and to my dear friend Carleton Varney whose friendship and guidance throughout this project is forever appreciated and remembered.

– Emberli Pridham

Once there was a girl named Grace Kelly,

a beautiful child with blue eyes and blonde hair.

She loved to play dress-up, play-act, and pretend,

and everything she did, she did with flair.

Grace grew up in a stately home in Philadelphia,

with her parents, two sisters, and a brother.

Her father had won three Olympic gold medals,

but the physical education teacher was her mother.

With her mother and sisters, Grace modeled for charity,

and at Ravenhill Academy, she found acting fun.

She played the lead in Don't Feed the Animals,

but her life as an actress had only just begun.

Grace excelled at drama and dance, truly loving her time on the stage. But her sights were set on Hollywood;

in her life, she was ready to turn the page.

Like her idols, Joseph Cotton and Ingrid Bergman,

Grace dreamed of being on the silver screen.

Her parents were worried, but Grace had a dream.

With the help of her Uncle George, Grace got into the American Academy of Dramatic Arts.

She used a tape recorder to improve her voice
   to ensure she sounded polished and smart.

Grace acted in The Philadelphia Story
   when she graduated at the end of the year.

It was a play named after her hometown,
   and the audience applauded and cheered!

$\mathcal{I}$n New York City, Grace modeled and acted in commercials, along with many TV shows and Broadway plays.

After that, the movies came calling.

Grace's career was ready for its next phase.

Grace co-starred in High Noon with Gary Cooper.

It was a big hit and got Grace much attention.

Little did she know, it would be the first film of many,

and she'd eventually win an Oscar and get another nomination!

Then Grace starred in Rear Window with Jimmy Stewart,

for a famous director named Alfred Hitchcock.

Now, when people saw Grace Kelly's name in lights,

they lined up around the block!

$\mathcal{H}$itchcock then cast Grace in To Catch a Thief,

where she dazzled in beautiful dresses.

She shared the screen with handsome Cary Grant,

and became one of Hollywood's most famous actresses.

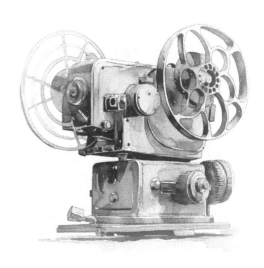

The next year, Grace starred in High Society.

Frank Sinatra and Bing Crosby tried to win her heart.

It was a remake of The Philadelphia Story, filmed in Newport, Rhode Island.

Back in school, she had played the same part!

While celebrating High Society at a film festival in France, Grace got the thrill of her life.

She met the Prince of Monaco at his beautiful palace,

and, after a year, he asked if she would be his wife.

Grace and Prince Rainier got married in a beautiful cathedral in Monaco.

Her wedding dress was exquisite and glamorous,

taking thirty-five dressmakers six weeks to sew!

The wedding ceremony was watched on TV

by thirty million people around the world.

And when Grace and Rainier took their vows,

everywhere ringing bells could be heard.

$\mathcal{W}$ithin just a few years,

Princess Grace became the mother of three.

She loved all her children very much,

Caroline, Albert, and Stephanie.

$\mathcal{P}$rincess Grace devoted her life
to helping others.

She became President of the Red
Cross of Monaco

and Patron of the Rainbow Coalition
Children

so kids everywhere could succeed
and grow.

At Christmas, Princess Grace gave orphaned children

many lovely and beautiful presents.

She hosted a party where they would all gather

and celebrate fun holiday events.

*P*rincess Grace also founded AMADE Mondiale,

aiding children from many countries.

And she helped lots of other charities and foundations

to protect young ones from hunger and disease.

$\mathcal{B}$ut Princess Grace still loved those working in the arts

for whom she formed the Princess Grace Foundation.

And she created the Princess Grace Academy at the Monte Carlo Ballet,

which thrived thanks to her generous donation.

In 1981, Princess Grace along with her son Prince Albert, were invited to Prince Charles and Princess Diana's wedding.

They were married in London's St. Paul's Cathedral,

which made quite a beautiful setting.

As Princess, Grace remained an icon of fashion.

Her Hermes purse was called the "Kelly bag" thanks to her popularity.

She created a fine linen brand called GPK, and donated her earnings to charity.

Though Hollywood wanted her back to star in one film after another, Princess Grace chose to stay at home and be a humanitarian, wife, and mother. Prince Rainier formed an American branch of her foundation to help artists working in film, dance, and the theater.

He wanted everyone to know what Grace always said:

"I would like to be remembered as a kind and loving person who did her best to help others."

Emberli Pridham grew up in Dallas, Texas inspired by her grandmother, an author, and a wonderful library of books. She, along with her husband David, are the co-authors of the Amazon best-selling STEM book series, *If Not You, Then Who?*, which aims to teach children about the inventions and patents in everyday life, inspiring and empowering them to imagine and create their own.

Emberli is currently writing the next two books about inspiring and influential people for the *Real Life Fairy Tale* series. She also spends her time taking care of her beautiful family and is extensively involved in philanthropic work on behalf of the Hasbro Children's Hospital, Dallas Museum of Art, Dallas Symphony, Elton John AIDS Foundation, and American Cancer Society, among other charities.

The Pridhams live and split their time between Texas and Rhode Island with their three ever-curious children Brooke, Noah, and Graham.

For more information visit areallifefairytale.com
Follow on Instagram @reallifefairytaleseries